ABOUT THE AUTHOR

Neil Ardley has written a number of innovative
nonfiction books for children, including *The
Eyewitness Guide to Music*. He also worked closely
with David Macaulay on *The Way Things Work*. In
addition to being a well-known author in the fields
of science, technology, and music, he is an
accomplished musician who composes and
performs both jazz and electronic music. He lives
in Derbyshire, England, with his wife and daughter.

Project Editors Scott Steedman and Laura Buller
Art Editors Mark Regardsoe and Earl Neish
Production Louise Barratt
Photography Dave King
Created by Dorling Kindersley Limited, London

Library of Congress Cataloging-in-Publication Data
Ardley, Neil.
The science book of machines / Neil Ardley.—1st U.S. ed.
p. cm.
"Gulliver books."
Summary: Simple experiments illustrate mechanical principles.
ISBN 0-15-200613-3
1. Mechanical engineering—Experiments—Juvenile literature.
[1. Mechanical engineering—Experiments. 2. Experiments.] I. Title.
TJ147.A73 1992
621'.078—dc20 91-20582

Printed in Belgium by Proost
First U.S. edition 1992
A B C D E

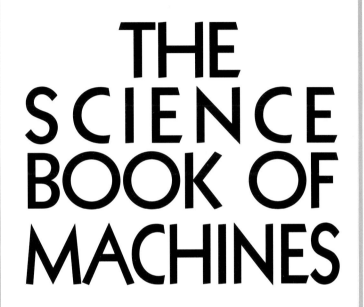

THE SCIENCE BOOK OF MACHINES

Neil Ardley

Gulliver Books

Harcourt Brace Jovanovich, Publishers

San Diego   New York   London

What are machines?

Machines are devices that do jobs for people. Some are small and simple, like a bottle opener or a pair of scissors. Others are large and complicated, like trains and cranes. Machines can help you do a job faster or make it easier. They can lift or move things and do jobs you could not do by yourself. Some machines are operated by hand; others are powered by engines or motors.

Machines that move you
Steam locomotives were the first machines to make quick long-distance travel possible.

Can-do device
This machine opens cans easily and safely. When you grip the handles, the blade is forced into the lid. Turning the other handle slices it open.

Uplifting machine
You can lift a car all by yourself if you use a jack. When you turn its crank, the jack pushes upward. It pushes with much more force than you use to turn the handle.

Smart machine

All you have to do to make this washing machine clean your laundry is turn it on. It is automatic—that is, it works under its own control.

A machine to count on

A calculator is a small, very complex device that helps you solve math problems quickly.

Nonstop workers

Robots are machines that can be "taught" to copy human movements and do jobs that people find boring or dangerous. Robots can also operate other machines, such as paint sprayers or welding torches.

⚠ This is a warning symbol. It appears within experiments next to steps that require caution. When you see this symbol, ask an adult for help.

Be a safe scientist
Follow all the instructions carefully and always use caution, especially with glass, scissors, matches, and sharp objects.

Never put anything into your mouth or eyes. Treat the machines you make with care. They may break and hurt you or others if you make them work too fast or too hard.

Load lifter

You can build a wheelbarrow, which works as a lever, to move a heavy load of stones. Using a lever lets you move things with less effort.

You will need:

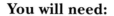

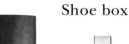
Two sticks of equal length

Stones

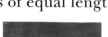
Plastic bag

Short pencil

Shoe box

Tape

Piece of cardboard

Thread spool

Scissors

1 Put the stones in the bag and lift them. It takes a lot of effort.

2 Tape the cardboard inside the box to make two sections.

Angle the sticks slightly.

3 Tape the sticks firmly to the bottom of the box.

The spool should just fit between the front ends.

4 Stick the pencil through the spool and tape it between the sticks at the front end. This is your wheelbarrow.

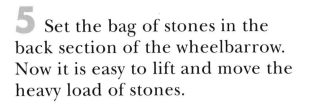

5 Set the bag of stones in the back section of the wheelbarrow. Now it is easy to lift and move the heavy load of stones.

The lever moves around the wheel.

The wooden sticks form a lever. The effort of your hands raises the end of the lever.

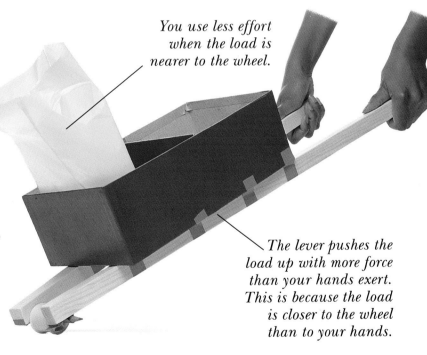

You use less effort when the load is nearer to the wheel.

6 Move the bag of stones to the front section. Now the heavy load is even easier to lift and move.

The lever pushes the load up with more force than your hands exert. This is because the load is closer to the wheel than to your hands.

Strong-arm tactic
A wrench gives you the strength you need to tighten a nut. It works as a lever. The movement you make to turn the handle becomes a shorter but more powerful movement at the other end.

Grain elevator

You can lift some cereal out of a bowl with the help of a lifting machine called an auger. An auger uses a screw to raise things up a tube.

You will need:

Rod

Tape

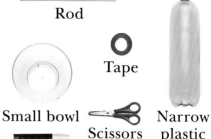
Narrow plastic bottle

Thin cardboard

Large bowl of puffed grain cereal

Small bowl

Pen

Scissors

1 ⚠ Ask an adult to cut both ends off the bottle to make a tube that is slightly shorter than the rod.

2 Use the tube to draw six bi circles on the cardboard.

3 Use the rod to draw a small circle in the center of each big circle. Cut out the large circles. Then cut across to the small ones and cut them out.

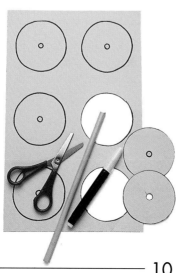

Tape a cut edge of each to the opposite cut edge of the circle below.

4 Tape the circles together, one on top of another.

10

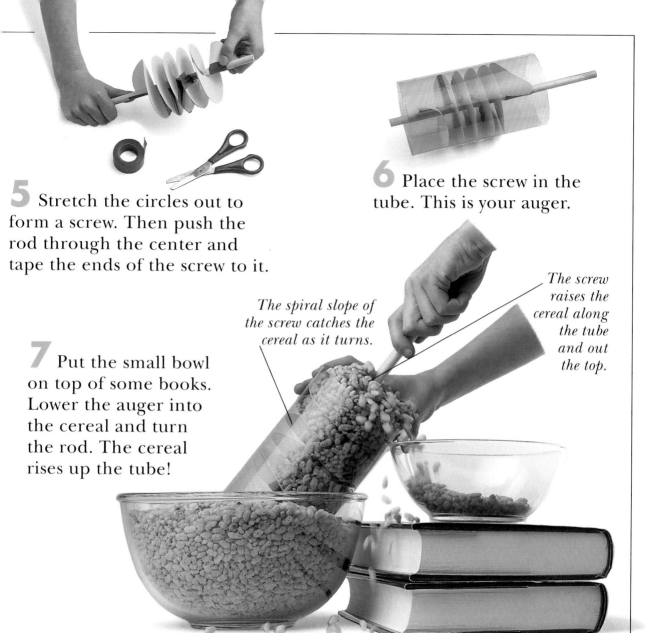

5 Stretch the circles out to form a screw. Then push the rod through the center and tape the ends of the screw to it.

6 Place the screw in the tube. This is your auger.

7 Put the small bowl on top of some books. Lower the auger into the cereal and turn the rod. The cereal rises up the tube!

The spiral slope of the screw catches the cereal as it turns.

The screw raises the cereal along the tube and out the top.

Gathering grain
A combine cuts wheat and removes the grain at the same time. Inside are several augers, one of which moves the loose grain up a chute and into a truck.

Sort it out

You can build a machine that separates large marbles from small ones. It is an automatic machine, which means it works under its own control.

You will need:

Straw

Thin wooden stick

 Two short cardboard boxes

 Glue

Large and small pieces of cardboard

One long cardboard box

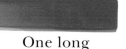 Large and small marbles

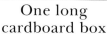 Tape

Scissors

Modeling clay

Openings

Make sure all three boxes are the same height.

Openings

1 Ask an adult to help you cut openings in the long box and in one of the short boxes. Glue them together.

2 Fold the small piece of cardboard lengthwise to make a chute. Attach it to the top of the other short box with clay.

Use a small piece of clay on this end, and a large piece on the other end.

To make a gutter, crease the edge of the cardboard twice.

3 Make a gutter on each side of the large piece of cardboard. Turn it over and tape the straw to the middle of it. Slide the stick through the straw.

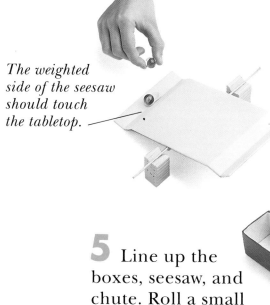

The weighted side of the seesaw should touch the tabletop.

4 Stick two small marbles into the middle of one of the gutters with clay. Balance the stick on two blocks of clay. This is your seesaw.

Make the clay supports tall enough so that the empty gutter lines up with the hole in the top box.

5 Line up the boxes, seesaw, and chute. Roll a small marble down the chute. It rolls across the gutter and into the upper box.

A small marble is not heavy enough to tilt the seesaw.

Use clay to raise the bottom of the chute if it does not line up with the seesaw and boxes.

Big marbles are heavy enough to tilt the seesaw.

6 Roll a heavy marble down the chute. The seesaw tilts, and the marble goes into the lower box.

Mail machine
This machine reads the postal codes on envelopes and automatically sorts them according to where they have to go.

Wind and whirl

How can you turn one spool and cause four to spin? By using a belt, you will see how some machines carry motion from one moving part to others.

You will need:

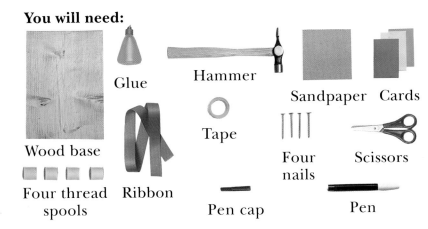

Wood base

Glue

Hammer

Sandpaper   Cards

Tape

Four thread spools   Ribbon

Pen cap

Four nails   Scissors

Pen

1 Cut four strips of sandpaper and glue them around the spools.

2 Arrange the spools on the base as shown.

Each spool should turn easily.

3 ⚠ Ask an adult to hammer a nail through the center hole of each spool.

Pull the ribbon tight before you tape the ends.

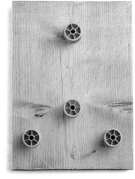

4 Loop the ribbon around the spools. Tape the ends together. Insert the pen cap into the top spool.

6 Insert the arrows into the three bottom spools.

5 Draw arrows (as shown) on the three cards and cut them out.

The ribbon is a belt. Turning the handle moves the belt, making all the spools turn.

7 Using the pen cap as a handle, turn the top spool. The three arrows spin around.

The middle arrow whirls in a direction opposite that of the other two arrows because the belt turns it from the opposite side of the spool.

Round and round

Beating eggs is easy with this machine. When the handle is cranked, the motion is transferred to two wheels. These wheels whirl the beaters in opposite directions so that they beat the eggs well.

Jump for joy

Make a figure jump up and down by turning a handle. You can do this with a machine that changes a circular motion into an up-and-down movement.

You will need:

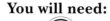
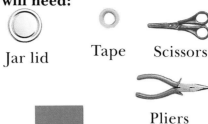

Jar lid

Tape

Scissors

Shoe box with lid

Pliers

Metal knitting needle

Drinking straw

Index card

Pen

Thin stick

1 ⚠ Push the knitting needle through the front of the box, just below the center.

2 ⚠ Ask an adult to bend the point of the knitting needle. Tape it to the inside of the lid.

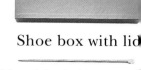

Cover the point with tape.

Place the bend against the bottom edge of the lid.

Rotate the lid to its highest position.

3 ⚠ Ask an adult to bend the other end of the knitting needle to form a handle.

4 Cut a short piece of straw. Tape it to the box above the lid.

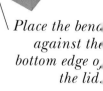

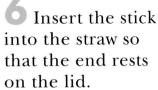

5 Draw a figure on the index card. Cut it out and tape it to the stick.

6 Insert the stick into the straw so that the end rests on the lid.

The lid turns on an off-center axle (the needle) so that its rotation covers a large area.

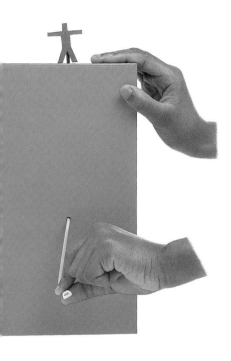

At the high point of the turn, the lid raises the stick; at the lowest point, the lid lets the stick fall.

7 Turn the handle. The figure jumps up and down.

Engine power
In this engine, powerful jets of steam push a long piston rod back and forth. Links, called cranks, connect the piston rod to the wheels. The cranks change the back-and-forth movement into a circular motion to make the wheels turn around.

Keeping cool

You can keep cool with a hand-powered fan. This machine uses a gear. The gear makes the fan spin faster than the handle you use to turn it. Gears allow parts of machines to work at different speeds.

You will need:

Thin wooden stick

Hammer

Knife

Thumbtack

Scissors

Box

Paper fastener

Nail

Three corks   Stiff plastic

Rubber band

Jar lid

Put the holes about 5 cm (2 in.) from the top and bottom of the box.

Put one hole in the middle of the lid and another hole toward the edge.

2 Push the thumbtack through the hole in the side of the lid. Stick a cork onto the tack. This is the handle.

1 ⚠ Ask an adult to make two holes near the top and bottom of the box. Turn the box over and make a third hole directly opposite the top hole. Make two holes in the jar lid.

Attach the handle to the bottom hole. The handle should turn easily.

3 Attach the handle to the box with the paper fastener

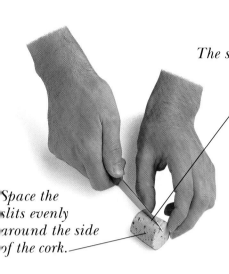

The slits should be slanted a little.

Space the slits evenly around the side of the cork.

4 ⚠ Ask an adult to cut four slits in one of the corks.

5 Cut four long strips from the plastic. Each one should be as wide as the slits in the cork.

The stick should be long enough to come out the other side of the box.

6 ⚠ Slide the strips into the slits in the cork to form the blades of the fan. Push one end of the stick into the cork.

7 Insert the stick through the top hole in the box and push it out through the hole in the opposite side.

Continued on next page

8 Push the other cork onto the uncovered end of the stick. Loop the rubber band around the cork and the jar lid. This is your fan.

The rubber band should fit without much stretching.

One wheel driving another is called a gear. Here, a belt (the rubber band) links the two wheels (the lid and the cork).

The blades spin faster than the handle turns. This is because the jar lid is a bigger wheel than the cork that it drives.

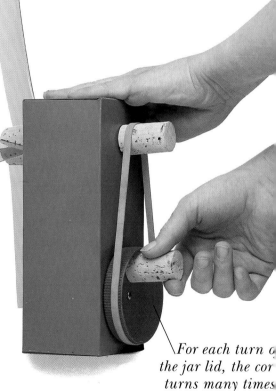

9 Wind the handle of the fan. The blades spin rapidly and push air forward.

For each turn of the jar lid, the cork turns many times.

Speedy ride
Gears help you to pedal a bicycle. The chain turns toothed gears on the back wheel. The smaller gears turn the wheel many times for each turn of the pedal.

Continued from previous page

Ball bearing

Parts of machines can rub together as they move. The rubbing, called friction, slows the machine down. Make a ball bearing and see how it reduces friction.

You will need:

Scissors

Two jar lids, one larger than the other

Marbles

Pencil

Tape

Modeling clay

1 Tape the pencil across the top of the larger lid. Then, using some clay, stick the smaller lid to a tabletop.

2 Place the larger lid over the smaller lid and spin it. The top lid hardly moves.

Friction between the lids stops them from spinning well.

3 Now put some marbles inside the small lid.

The marbles should roll easily and be large enough to keep the lids apart.

The rolling marbles reduce the friction.

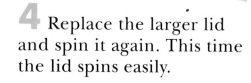

4 Replace the larger lid and spin it again. This time the lid spins easily.

Spool racer

Many machines are powered by motors. Motors can be complex, such as the engines in cars, or very simple, such as the rubber-band motor that drives the racer in this experiment.

Use two rubber bands on each side.

1 Wind four of the rubber bands around the thread spool to make two tires.

2 Thread the fifth rubber band through the center of the spool. Loop the end of the rubber band around the matchstick. Tape the matchstick to the spool.

3 ⚠ Ask an adult to make a hole in the bottle cap.

The rubber band should be tight. Knot the band if it is too long.

4 Push the other end of the rubber band through the hole in the cap. Slip the knitting needle through the rubber band.

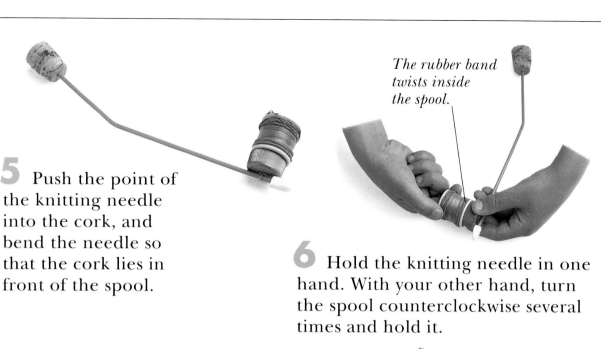

The rubber band twists inside the spool.

5 Push the point of the knitting needle into the cork, and bend the needle so that the cork lies in front of the spool.

6 Hold the knitting needle in one hand. With your other hand, turn the spool counterclockwise several times and hold it.

7 Set the spool on the floor and let it go. It races across the room.

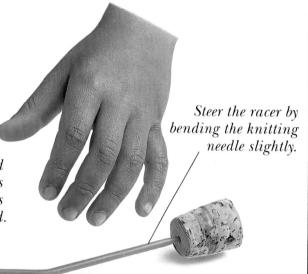

Steer the racer by bending the knitting needle slightly.

As the rubber band untwists, it turns the spool and pulls the racer forward.

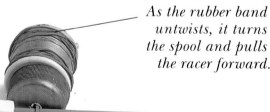

Driving force

This motorcycle changes the power an engine produces into forward movement. The engine turns a gear that is attached by a chain to the back wheel. The wheel turns with enough force to push the motorcycle forward.

Waterworks

Can you raise a heavy weight with just a little water? By building your own "hydraulic" machine, you can use water to lift a weight.

You will need:

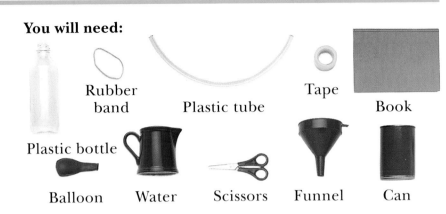

Rubber band

Plastic tube

Tape

Book

Plastic bottle

Balloon

Water

Scissors

Funnel

Can

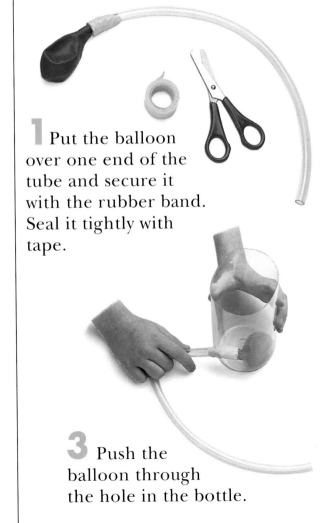

1 Put the balloon over one end of the tube and secure it with the rubber band. Seal it tightly with tape.

2 ⚠ Ask an adult to cut the top off the plastic bottle and to cut a hole in the side of the bottle, near the base.

3 Push the balloon through the hole in the bottle.

4 Tape the funnel to the end of the tube.

24

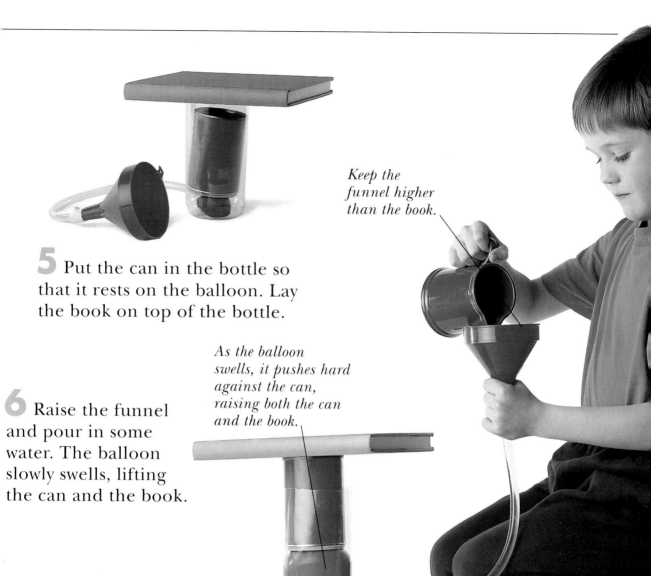

Keep the funnel higher than the book.

5 Put the can in the bottle so that it rests on the balloon. Lay the book on top of the bottle.

As the balloon swells, it pushes hard against the can, raising both the can and the book.

6 Raise the funnel and pour in some water. The balloon slowly swells, lifting the can and the book.

The weight of the water in the tube pushes the water into the balloon.

Big digger

Construction excavators use hydraulics. Liquid is pumped into cylinders, where it pushes out pistons. The pistons can force the bucket into the ground and also raise heavy loads of soil.

Pulley power

Pulling weight downward feels easier than lifting it up. A pulley changes a downward pull into an upward lift. You can build a model crane that uses a pulley to lift a heavy load.

You will need:

 Pen cap

Paper clip

Scissors

Two nails

 Marbles

Plastic cup

Two thread spools

 String   Tape   Hammer

 Piece of wood

Sturdy cardboard box

 Book

Position the spools on the wood as shown.

1 ⚠️ Ask an adult to nail the two spools to the wood. The spools should be able to turn easily.

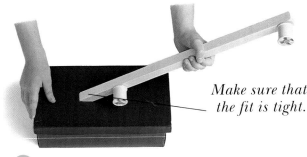

Make sure that the fit is tight.

2 Cut a hole in the box. Insert the wood so that it sticks out at an angle.

3 Cut a short piece of string. Tape the ends to the cup like the handle on a bucket.

4 Push the pen cap into the lower spool to form a handle. Tape the remaining string to this spool.

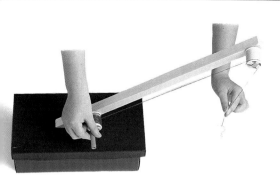

6 Open the paper clip and bend it into a hook. Tie it to the other end of the string.

5 Loop the string over the top spool. Then hold the string taut while you wind it onto the bottom spool.

The upper spool is a pulley. It changes the downward force of the handle into an upward force that lifts the load.

Place a book on the box. This is a counterweight. It prevents the load from pulling the crane over.

7 Fill the cup with marbles and hook it to the crane. Then wind the handle to lift the cup.

High-rise machine
A tower crane has a tall arm called a boom that lowers a hook to the load. As the crane raises or lowers the load, the boom swivels around to move the load sideways. A huge concrete counterweight prevents the crane from toppling over.

Tug-of-war

You can increase your strength with a set of pulleys. Use them to pull two people together, even though they struggle to stay apart!

Two broom handles

Long piece of rope

1 Ask a friend to hold a broom handle with both hands. Tie the rope to it.

2 Ask another friend to hold the other handle and to stand opposite your first friend.

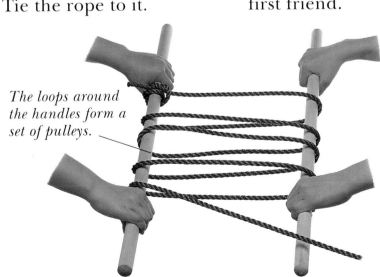

The loops around the handles form a set of pulleys.

3 Loop the rope around the broom handles several times.

28

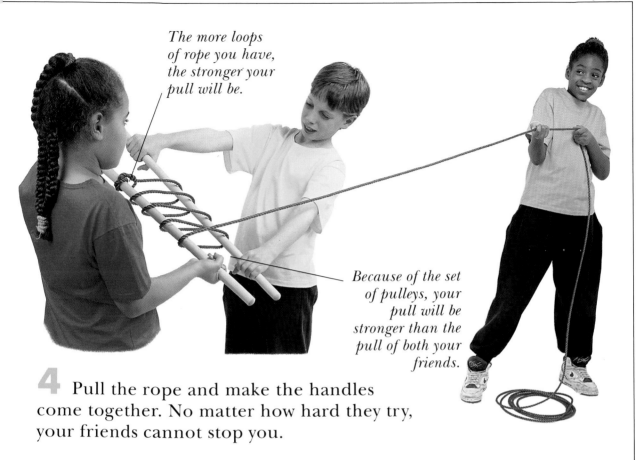

The more loops of rope you have, the stronger your pull will be.

Because of the set of pulleys, your pull will be stronger than the pull of both your friends.

4 Pull the rope and make the handles come together. No matter how hard they try, your friends cannot stop you.

Pulling power
The set of pulleys on the end of this crane is called a block and tackle. Just one cable passes around the pulleys. The block and tackle can lift a heavy load with just a light pull on the cable.

Picture credits
(Picture credits abbreviation key: B=below, C=center, L=left, R=right, T=top)

Robert Harding Picture Library/Ian Griffiths: 23BL; Christopher D. Howson: 6BL; The Image Bank: 11BL, 13BL; The Image Bank/Al Satterwhite: 25BR; The Image Bank/Jurgen Voight: 27BL; Pictor International: 17BL; Science Photo Library/David Parker/600 Group: 7C; Tony Stone Worldwide/Jon Riley: 29C; Zefa Picture Library: 7TL; Zefa Picture Library/M. Mehltretter: 6TL.

Picture research Kathy Lockley and Clive Webster

Science consultant Jack Challoner

Dorling Kindersley would like to thank Jenny Vaughan for editorial assistance; Mrs Bradbury, Mr Millington, the staff and children of Allfarthing Junior School, Wandsworth, especially Daniel Armstrong, Gemma Bradford, Lucy Gibson, Keisha McLeod, Kate Miller, Sonia Opong, Ben Sells, Cheryl Small, Ruth Tross, Duncan Warren, Kate Ling, Lori Randall, Luke Randall, and Kristy Gould.

DEMCO